Upright Bass

Matilda James

xist Publishing

A Note to Parents & Teachers—

Welcome to Discover Musical Instruments from Xist Publishing! These books are designed to inspire discovery and delight in the youngest readers. Each short book features very simple sentences with visual cues to get kids reading for the first time.

You can help each child develop a lifetime love of reading right from the very start. Here are some ways to help a beginning reader get going:

- Read the book aloud as a first introduction
- Run your fingers below the words as you read each line
- Give the child the chance to finish the sentences or read repeating words while you read the rest.
- Encourage the child to read aloud every day!

First Edition

Published in the United States by Xist Publishing
www.xistpublishing.com
24200 Southwest Freeway #402-290 Rosenberg, TX 77471

eISBN: 978-1-5324-1715-3
Paperback ISBN: 978-1-5324-1716-0
Hardcover ISBN: 978-1-5324-1717-7

Table of Contents

This is an upright bass.

The upright bass is a string instrument.

Upright basses are made of wood.

Upright basses have four strings.

I play the
upright bass
with my fingers
and a bow.

I press on the strings
to change the sound.

Upright basses play very low notes.

Upright basses can be part of an orchestra.

I can play the upright bass in a group or by myself.

I like to play the upright bass.

Photo Glossary

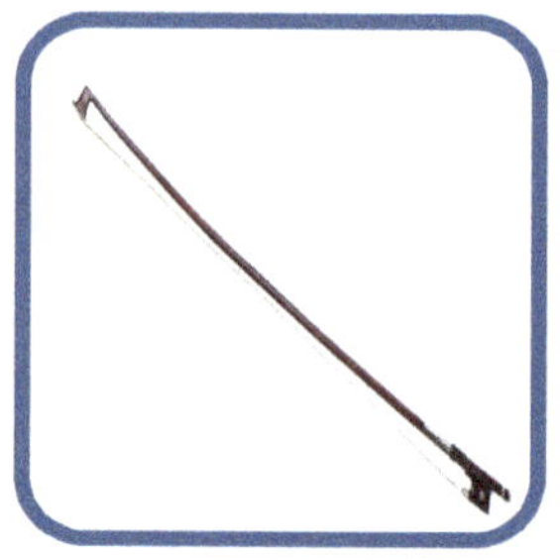

Bow

Curved piece of wood used for playing a string instrument

Orchestra

A group of musicians who play together

Strings

Thin pieces of metal or other material that make sound

Wood

Hard material from a tree

Things to do next!

Write a Sentence

Upright bass are ___________.

Drawing

Draw yourself playing an upright bass.

Sharing

Tell your classmates about a musical instrument you have heard.

Index

www.ingramcontent.com/pod-product-compliance
Ingram Content Group UK Ltd.
Pitfield, Milton Keynes, MK11 3LW, UK
UKHW062300290726
14090UKWH00017B/799